Contents

What Is a Robbery? 4–5

Great Brink's Robbery 6–7

Mona Lisa is Missing! 8–9

Dunbar Armoured Robbery 10–11

Knightsbridge Security Deposit Robbery 12–13

Lufthansa Robbery 14–15

Northern Bank Robbery 16–17

Brink's Mat Robbery 18–19

Gardner Museum 20–21

Millennium Dome Diamonds 22–23

The Scream 24–25

Bank Robbery in Brazil 26–27

Computer Criminals 28–29

Glossary 30

Want to Know More? 31

Index 32

Some words are printed in bold, **like this**. You can find out what they mean in the glossary. You can also look in the box at the bottom of the page where the word first appears.

WHAT IS A ROBBERY?

A robbery is a serious crime. Robberies can happen anywhere. There are robberies at banks. There are robberies at airports and museums. In a robbery, **valuable** things are stolen.

Teams for trouble!

Robbers often work together in a gang. They usually try to steal money, but sometimes they steal jewellery and works of art. They plan their crimes carefully. Robbers try to leave no clues.

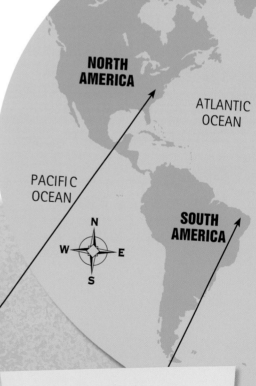

NORTH AMERICA

ATLANTIC OCEAN

PACIFIC OCEAN

SOUTH AMERICA

N
W   E
S

John F. Kennedy International Airport, New York: Lufthansa Robbery
(see page 15)

Fortaleza, Brazil: Bank Robbery in Brazil
(see page 26)

ATOMIC

ERIES

Raintree

www.raintreepublishers.co.uk
Visit our website to find out more information about **Raintree** books.

To order:
- ☎ Phone 44 (0) 1865 888112
- 📄 Send a fax to 44 (0) 1865 314091
- 💻 Visit the Raintree bookshop at **www.raintreepublishers.co.uk** to browse our catalogue and order online.

First published in Great Britain by Raintree, Halley Court, Jordan Hill, Oxford OX2 8EJ, part of Harcourt Education. Raintree is a registered trademark of Harcourt Education Ltd.

© Harcourt Education Ltd 2008
First published in paperback in 2008.
The moral right of the proprietor has been asserted.

Editorial: Louise Galpine and Catherine Clarke
Design: Victoria Bevan and Bigtop
Picture research: Hannah Taylor
Illustrations: Jeff Edwards
Production: Julie Carter

Originated by Chroma Graphics Pte. Ltd
Printed and bound in China by Leo Paper Group

ISBN: 978 1 4062 0672 2 (hardback)
12 11 10 09 08
10 9 8 7 6 5 4 3 2 1

ISBN: 978 1 4062 0693 7 (paperback)
13 12 11 10 09
10 9 8 7 6 5 4 3 2 1

**British Library
Cataloguing in Publication Data**
Weil, Ann
Robberies. – (True stories) (Atomic)
364.1'552
A full catalogue record for this book is available from the British Library.

Acknowledgements
The publishers would like to thank the following for permission to reproduce photographs: Alamy Images pp. **6** (Dennis MacDonald), **13** (top) (David Young-Wolff), **14** (bottom) (Digital Archive Japan), **29** (MM_Photo); Corbis pp. **10** (top) (Royalty Free), **13** (bottom) (John Wilkes Studio), **20** (Brooks Kraft); Daily News Pix p. **14** (top); Empics (AP) p. **19** (top); Getty Images pp. **9**, **27** (AFP); Los Angeles Times (Genaro Molina) p. **10** (bottom); Munch Museum/Munch– Ellingsen Group, BONO, Oslo, DACS, London 2006 Photo: 1990, Photo Scala, Florence/ Nasjonalgalleriet p. **24**; Reuters pp. **16** (Handout MD), **23** (top) (Russell Boyce); Rex Features pp. **19** (bottom), **23** (bottom).

Cover photograph of a masked robber reproduced with permission of Corbis (Tom Grill).

The publishers would like to thank Diana Bentley, Nancy Harris, and Dee Reid for their assistance in the preparation of this book.

Every effort has been made to contact copyright holders of any material reproduced in this book. Any omissions will be rectified in subsequent printings if notice is given to the publishers.

Disclaimer
All the Internet addresses (URLs) given in this book were valid at the time of going to press. However, due to the dynamic nature of the Internet, some addresses may have changed, or sites may have changed or ceased to exist since publication. While the author and publishers regret any inconvenience this may cause readers, no responsibility for any such changes can be accepted by either the author or the publishers.

Paris, France:

Mona Lisa is Missing!

(see page 8)

Oslo, Norway:

The Scream

(see page 25)

ARCTIC OCEAN

EUROPE

ASIA

AFRICA

Robberies can happen all over the world. We are going to look at the robberies shown on this map and more!

PACIFIC OCEAN

INDIAN OCEAN

AUSTRALIA

SOUTHERN OCEAN

ANTARCTICA

valuable   worth a lot of money

Brink's armoured trucks carry large amounts of money to and from buildings. The robbery took place at the Brink's depot.

Amazing facts!

The gang members wore Halloween masks to hide their faces.

GREAT BRINK'S ROBBERY

17 January 1950
Brink's Building
Boston, Massachusetts, USA

A gang of robbers planned everything. They had the keys they needed to get inside the Brink's Building **depot**. Once they were inside, they tied up the workers. They stole more than £1.3 million and left few clues.

Crime solved

After the robbery, the police kept track of **suspects**. Some suspects ended up in jail for other crimes. Finally, the police solved the crime and the robbers went to jail. However, most of the money was never found.

depot	**building for storing things**
suspect	**someone police believe may be guilty of a crime**

Mona Lisa is Missing!

21 August 1911
The Louvre Museum
Paris, France

Vincenzo Perugia worked at the Louvre. One night he hid in the museum after work. He took the famous painting the *Mona Lisa* out of its frame. He hid it under his clothes and left the museum.

Lost and found

The next day, workers saw that the painting was missing. They thought someone had simply moved the painting. It took another day for people to realize it was stolen!

Police had no clues. Then, more than two years later, the painting was seen. Perugia showed it to an art dealer in Italy. The dealer told the police, and Perugia was arrested.

The *Mona Lisa* was painted by artist Leonardo da Vinci. It is now kept behind security glass at the Louvre.

Amazing facts!

The Dunbar robbery became the largest cash robbery in US history.

DUNROB TASK FORCE

FEDERAL BUREAU OF INVESTIGATION

LOS ANGELES POLICE DEPARTMENT

IF YOU'
WANTED
BY THE F
LOS ANGELE
BANK SQUAD

HIDE.

The FBI had a special team investigating the Dunbar robbery.

DUNBAR ARMOURED ROBBERY

13 September 1997
Dunbar Armoured **Depot**
Los Angeles, California, USA

Allen Pace worked at the Dunbar Armoured depot. He let robbers hide in the cafeteria. The robbers surprised the guards and tied them up. Then, they got away with nearly £9.7 million in cash.

Following clues

The police knew it was an **inside job**, but they needed proof. A broken tail light was found at the crime scene. This led police to a rented truck. The man who rented the truck gave police more information. They used this to find the robbers and solve the crime.

| inside job | crime involving someone who works for the people being robbed |

KNIGHTSBRIDGE SECURITY DEPOSIT ROBBERY

12 July 1987
Knightsbridge Safe Deposit Centre
London

Two men asked to rent a safe deposit box. A guard took them inside the vault.

No safe is safe

The men pulled out their guns. They hung a "Closed" sign on the door. Then they let in members of their group. They took money and goods worth about £34 million.

After the robbers left, one of the guards got out of his handcuffs and called the police. The police found a fingerprint. It belonged to one of the robbers. This led to his arrest.

safe deposit box
vault

locked drawer inside a bank
locked room in a bank

A safe deposit box keeps money and **valuable** items safe.

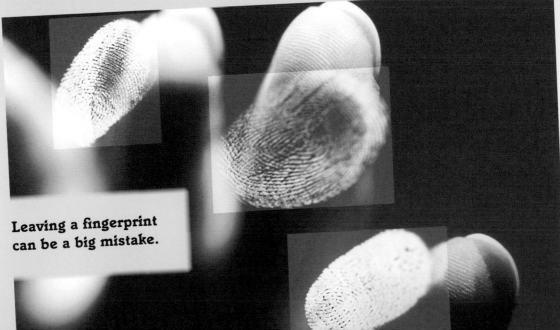

Leaving a fingerprint can be a big mistake.

This van was used by the robbers to carry their loot.

cargo	goods that are shipped by air, land, or sea
cargo terminal	place where cargo is stored at the airport
loot	stolen money or goods

LUFTHANSA ROBBERY

11 December 1978
Lufthansa **Cargo Terminal**
John F. Kennedy International
Airport, New York, USA

Aeroplanes fly from place to place with people and cargo on board. When the cargo arrives it is stored at a terminal.

Dead men can't talk!

Sometimes cargo is money. A gang of robbers stole £2.5 million in cash from an airport cargo terminal. They also got £436,000 worth of jewellery. One of the robbers worked at the airport. He was later caught and sent to prison. The police had other **suspects**, but no proof.

In the years after the crime, many of these suspects were murdered! The killer was probably the one who planned the robbery. This way, no one could give his name to the police.

NORTHERN BANK ROBBERY

20 December 2004
Northern Bank Building
Belfast, Northern Ireland

Robbers forced this bank worker to leave with a bag of stolen money.

hostage	someone who is held prisoner

Sunday, 19 December 2004
10 p.m.

Three men wearing masks went to Chris Ward's house. Ward worked for Northern Bank. The men held Ward's family **hostage**. Then, they took Ward to his boss's house.

11.30 p.m.

The men tied up Ward's boss, Kevin McMullan, and McMullan's wife. Some of the men took Mrs. McMullan away as another hostage.

Monday, 20 December 2004
6.30 a.m.

The masked men gave Ward and McMullan their orders. They had to help the masked men rob the bank. If they did this, they would save their families.

12 noon

The bankers got to work.

7 p.m.

Ward and McMullan let the robbers into the bank. The robbers collected all the money and got away in a van.

11 p.m.

The hostages were released.

11.45 p.m.

The hunt for the robbers began.

BRINK'S MAT ROBBERY

26 November 1983
Brink's Mat Warehouse
Heathrow Airport, London

Six robbers broke into the Brink's Mat warehouse. They expected to find a lot of cash. But they did not expect to find 10 tonnes of gold! The robbers took it all.

Case closed

Soon after, the police solved the case. It was an **inside job**. The guard who helped the robbers get inside the warehouse **confessed**. Later, the police arrested the robbers and put them in jail.

confess   tell the truth

Amazing facts!

Three tonnes of the stolen gold was never found. That gold was probably made into jewellery. This means that many people could be wearing stolen jewellery and not even realize it!

Police set up a control room at the Brink's crime scene.

The empty frames of the stolen art hang on the walls of the Gardner Museum.

Amazing facts!

The museum offered a £2.5 million reward.

GARDNER MUSEUM

18 March 1990
Isabella Stewart Gardner Museum
Boston, Massachusetts, USA

Two men banged on the door of the Isabella Stewart Gardner Museum at 1.24 a.m. They wore police uniforms. The guards were not supposed to let anyone in. Still, they let the men inside. But the men were not really police. They were robbers.

Still missing

Once inside, the robbers tied up the guards. They then stole 13 works of art worth £154 million. It was one of the biggest art thefts in US history.

The police have never made any arrests. None of the art has been found.

MILLENNIUM DOME DIAMONDS

7 November 2000
Millennium Dome
Greenwich, London

Robbers in London spent months planning to steal diamonds on display at the Millennium Dome.

Simple plan

The robbers' plan was daring and simple:

1. Hide their faces with gas masks.
2. Use a bulldozer to smash their way into the Millennium Dome.
3. Break through the security glass protecting the display.
4. Steal 12 rare and **valuable** diamonds. This included the Millennium Star.
5. Escape down the River Thames in a fast boat.

But the police knew all about their plan.
They were waiting when the robbers arrived.

The Millennium Jewels

The robbers' bulldozer joined the diamonds on display!

You can see the Millennium Star through the smashed glass left by the robbers.

Amazing facts!

The pear-shaped Millennium Star is the third-largest diamond ever found.

Amazing facts!

The 2004 heist was the second time a version of *The Scream* had been stolen. The first time was in February 1994. The police found the painting several months later.

Edvard Munch painted more than one version of his famous painting *The Scream*.

THE SCREAM

22 August 2004
Munch Museum
Oslo, Norway

Two masked men walked into the Munch Museum. One robber pointed a gun at visitors and museum workers. The other tore paintings from the wall.

The artist Edvard Munch had made these paintings. One painting, called *The Scream*, was very famous. The two robbers escaped in a car driven by a third man.

Paintings back home

For two years the crime remained unsolved. Then, in 2006 police found the stolen paintings. They were once again put on display to the public.

heist   another word for "robbery"

BANK ROBBERY IN BRAZIL

The weekend of 6-7 August 2005
Banco Central
Fortaleza, Brazil

A group of men rented a house in Brazil. Every day vans took dirt away from the house.

Digging for cash

Neighbours thought this was part of a gardening business. However, the men were really digging a tunnel. It took them three months. The tunnel was about 75 metres (250 feet) long. It ended underneath a bank.

Finally, the robbers broke through concrete under the bank. They were inside the **vault**. The robbers took all the money from the vault back through the tunnel. The robbery was discovered on Monday morning. The police found and arrested some of the robbers. However, more than half of the money is still missing.

Neighbours didn't realize that robbers were digging this tunnel next door!

COMPUTER CRIMINALS

In the past, robbers used guns to steal. Now, bank robbers are just as likely to use a computer.

Computer **criminals** are called **hackers**. They steal passwords. Passwords are meant to protect computer files. Hackers break into a bank's computer files instead of its **vaults**. The result is the same. Millions of pounds are lost. The money is **transferred** (moved) to the criminals' bank accounts.

Identity theft

Identity theft is when criminals use someone else's personal information. They use it to get a credit card or loan. They get the money and the goods, but their victims are left with the bill.

criminal	person who breaks the law
hacker	computer criminal
transfer	move from one place to another

Hackers don't need masks or guns to rob banks. They just need a computer!

Glossary

cargo goods that are shipped by air, land, or sea

cargo terminal place where cargo is stored at the airport

confess tell the truth. Robbers sometimes confess to the police that they have stolen something.

criminal person who breaks the law. Robbers are criminals.

depot building for storing things

hacker computer criminal. Hackers "break into" computers.

heist another word for "robbery"

hostage someone who is held prisoner. Criminals use hostages to get what they want.

inside job crime involving someone who works for the people being robbed. If someone who works at a bank helps to rob it, it is an inside job.

loot stolen money or goods

safe deposit box locked drawer inside a bank. People can store valuable items in these boxes.

suspect someone police believe may be guilty of a crime

transfer move from one place to another

valuable worth a lot of money

vault locked room in a bank. Money and safe deposit boxes are kept in the vault.

Want to Know More?

Books

✳ *Forensic Files: Investigating Thefts and Heists*, Alex Woolf (Heinemann Library, 2005)

✳ *The Mona Lisa Caper*, Rick Jacobson (Tundra, 2005)

✳ *A Painful History of Crime: Crime Through Time*, John Townsend (Raintree, 2005)

Websites

✳ www.fbi.gov/kids/k5th/kidsk5th.htm
Have a look at the FBI's kids' site to see how they work to solve crimes.

✳ www.yahooligans.com
Try typing "Mona Lisa" into this search engine and follow the link to learn more about the theft of this great painting.

If you liked this Atomic book, why don't you try these...?

Index

armoured trucks 6
art thefts 4, 8–9, 20–21, 24–25

bank robberies 4, 16–17, 26–27
bank vaults 26
Brink's Building robbery 6–7
Brink's Mat Robbery 18–19
bulldozers 22, 23

computer criminals 28–29

diamonds 22, 23
Dunbar Armoured Depot robbery 10–11

fingerprints 12, 13
Fortaleza, Brazil 4, 26–27

gold 18, 19

hackers 28–29
hostages 16, 17

identity theft 28
inside jobs 11, 18
Isabella Stewart Gardner Museum 20–21

jewellery 4, 15, 19
John F. Kennedy International Airport 4, 15

Knightsbridge Security Deposit robbery
   12–13

Louvre, Paris 8–9
Lufthansa robbery 4, 14–15

masks 6, 17, 22, 25
Millennium Dome diamonds 22–23
Mona Lisa 5, 8–9
money 4, 6, 7, 10, 11, 12, 13, 15, 17, 26, 28

Northern Bank robbery 16–17

Pace, Allen 11
passwords 28

safe deposit boxes 12–13
Scream, The 5, 24–25
suspects 7, 15

tunnels 26, 27

Notes for adults

Use the following questions to guide children towards identifying features of recount text:

Can you give an example of scene setting from page 12?
Can you find a recount of events on page 17?
Can you find an example of a temporal connective on page 18?
Can you give examples of past tense language on page 21?
Can you give an example of a closing statement from page 26?